WORCESTERSHIRE

A portrait of the county

WORCESTERSHIRE

A portrait of the county

Photographs and design by
John Bradford

Text by
Sam Redgrave

Halfshire Books
6 High Street, Bromsgrove
Worcestershire B61 8HQ

First published in Great Britain
by Halfshire Books 1996

ISBN 1 899062 02 5 Hardback
ISBN 1 899062 03 3 Paperback

Acknowledgements

The publishers would like to thank those who helped in a variety of ways with the preparation of this book and to acknowledge in particular the following for their kind permission to reproduce illustrations:

Avoncroft Museum of Buildings (page 47)
Worcester Porcelain (page 18)
The Morgan Motor Company Ltd (page 73)

and Joe Hunt for permission to reproduce an extract from his poem
Severn (page 95)

Typeset by Avonset, St Chads Green, Midsomer Norton,
near Bath BA3 2JT.
Printed in Great Britain by Barwell Colour Print Ltd,
Midsomer Norton, near Bath BA3 4BS

(Page ii illustration) Thatched cottage at Great Comberton, one of a cluster of half-timbered villages nestling around the foot of Bredon

CONTENTS

FOREWORD

I write with real pride in Worcestershire - my county of wide fertile valleys, its great plain surrounded by hills which are never far away and give to the county a unity and wholeness. From north to south runs the River Severn, the ancient fluvial backbone, crucial in the industrial and commercial revolutions of the past. Now it is a great source of pleasure and recreation.

Out of diversity comes strength. Worcestershire is still two-thirds agricultural; but the market gardens of the Vale of Evesham give way to the old religious, commercial and administrative centre of Worcester; and further north is the former salt town of Droitwich Spa and other centres with a rich industrial heritage - carpets in Kidderminster, needles and fishing tackle at Redditch and nails and chains in Bromsgrove.

Worcestershire has a proud past. You cannot have a present without a past; and you cannot have a future without a present. It is our privilege to use and enjoy our inheritance - and our duty to safeguard it for future generations.

John Wardle

John Wardle MBE DL
Chairman, Hereford and Worcester County Council

(Above) Worcester Cathedral, from Fort Royal Park

(Opposite page) 16th-century sandstone bridge at Eckington, probably the most perfect of the county's old bridges

THE CITY OF WORCESTER

Worcester is one of England's finest shire towns, a vibrant mix of the old and new. Originally an important ford over the Severn, its beginnings can be traced to Roman times. By the middle ages it was a place of real importance, with a Norman cathedral built on the site of an earlier one, and a castle and walls which offered a measure of protection. In the 18th century it developed into an elegant regional capital, a renovated and rebuilt city of handsome houses, fashionable shops, well-paved streets and diverse entertainment.

In today's city there is ample evidence of these two thousand years of change: a cathedral with royal tombs and a beautifully recreated crypt; restored timber-framed houses, most put to modern use; a Civil War Trail marking the importance of the area in that conflict; a Georgian Guildhall, one of the finest in England; a handful of well-designed churches; some attractive industrial buildings; and the country's prettiest cricket ground.

Worcester has learned to respect and build on its past. Two of its old industries - porcelain and sauce - are still world famous; its theatre continues the strong tradition of three centuries; and its racecourse can look back over some three hundred years on Pitchcroft. Associated with the Three Choirs Festival, the oldest music festival in Europe, is Edward Elgar, the city's most famous son, whose modern statue stands at the boundary between cathedral precinct and bustling shops.

(Above) Crown Passage, next to a once great coaching inn, now a stylish place to shop and eat

(Opposite page) The Severn at Worcester. To the right, the cathedral tower, to the left, St Andrew's spire, the slenderest in the country

Worcester Cathedral owes its existence to a small band of missionaries from Whitby who raised a wooden church here over thirteen centuries ago. Today's building was consecrated by Bishop Wulstan in 1084 and is the result of additions and restoration carried out over the centuries. The recreated crypt, however, is almost as Wulstan built it, and among the cathedral's other notable features are the richly sculpted nave pulpit, the painted quire ceiling and the carved bosses in the cloisters. Two royal tombs are housed here. King John was carried from Newark in 1216 and buried where he wanted to be, before the high altar. The young Prince Arthur, Henry VII's eldest son, was conveyed in solemn procession from Ludlow where he had died shortly after marrying Katharine of Aragon. He lies in a specially built chantry in the south quire.

WORCESTER CATHEDRAL:
(Top right) the quire, a fine example of Norman architecture; (right) King John's tomb with the earliest royal effigy in England, a masterpiece of early-13th-century sculpture; (opposite page) the beautiful Early Norman crypt, restored in the 1980s

The Edgar Tower from College Green, on the left the former 18th-century deanery

Glimpsed from the High Street the cathedral stands on a busy junction, its precinct sliced into by a road built in 1792; but College Green gives a real feel of an old cathedral close. The Edgar Tower, once the castle entrance, was built for King John and named after King Edgar whose cross-legged figure sat for several centuries until it crumbled and was restored early this century. The Green underlines the historic intimacy between King's School and the cathedral. They stand facing each other, the one founded at the Reformation out of revenues once belonging to the other. The Edgar Tower houses the school library, the medieval refectory its hall and the former deanery its administrative office.

(Left) College Green: on the right the precentor's house

(Opposite page) College Precincts, just outside the cathedral's east wall

THE CITY OF WORCESTER

By the middle ages the ancient borough of Worcester was an important town with a prosperous cloth industry. Friar Street, with some of the finest timber-framed buildings, gives the best picture of how medieval Worcester must have looked. The street has had its ups and downs, and earlier this century even Greyfriars, its jewel, had become slum property. In recent years, however, conservation has been the watchword and Greyfriars is now in the care of the National Trust. The Guildhall, with its wonderfully decorated facade, symbolises the city's development in the 18th century into a thriving and elegant regional centre. It was begun in 1721 on the site of its predecessor and restored in the 1870s.

(Top right) The Guildhall, one of the finest town halls in the country

(Right) The cathedral, from the west bank of the Severn

(Opposite page) Friar Street with its wealth of black-and-white timber-framed buildings. On the left the beautifully restored building known as Greyfriars

Peaceful for much of its history, Worcestershire edged centre stage during the English Civil War. The city itself saw both the opening skirmish in 1642 and the final battle in 1651 fought mainly around Powick and on higher ground south-east of the walls. Only after a day of seesawing fortunes was Charles's army driven back by Cromwell's much larger forces: the dying Duke of Hamilton was carried back to the Commandery, serving as the Royalist headquarters, and by the Sidbury gate a thousand Scots were slaughtered as they sought shelter in the city. Charles was lodging in New Street where he fled on a borrowed horse after the battle, escaping out of the back and through St Martin's gate.

(Left) King Charles House, built by a rich 16th-century brewer and now a restaurant

(Opposite page) The Commandery, an impressive Tudor building on the site of the 11th-century Hospital of St Wulstan

The clock of St Swithun's, an 18th-century church with a perfect Georgian interior

Worcester is famous for its porcelain and sauce. A porcelain works was first established in 1751, following experiments into soft soapstone paste china by local physician John Wall and apothecary William Davis. Since then the company has diversified and adjusted to changing demand but the artistic and technical excellence of Royal Worcester Porcelain has never faltered. Worcestershire Sauce was first advertised as 'a sauce from the recipe of a Nobleman of Worcestershire'. The nobleman was Lord Sandys, lately returned from India, whose 'secret' the Broad Street chemists, John Lea and William Perrins, acquired in the 1820s.

(Left) A fine Victorian factory in Shrub Hill Road, built to construct engines and rolling stock for the railway

(Right) 'Medici' dinner set by Worcester Porcelain

(Right) Crown Gate shopping centre, echoing an emphasis on quality applauded two centuries ago

(Below) Worcestershire Sauce, its world-famous piquancy based on a 'secret' recipe

THE ABBERLEY HILLS
AND THE SEVERN VALLEY

ritain's longest river, the Severn, bisects this lovely area. Tidal and at times treacherous, a century and a half ago the river was one of Europe's leading commercial highways, bustling with traffic between Bristol and the Black Country. Pleasure boats and anglers after salmon are the river's users now; and it is tourists, rather than working boatmen, who visit the former Severn ports of Stourport and Georgian Bewdley.

Entering at Upper Arley, the Severn flows purposefully through the county towards the sea, passing on its west the ancient forest of Wyre, one of the country's most important broadleaved woodlands whose six thousand acres are home to a rich variety of wildlife. Further south, in farmland dotted with woods, are several large country houses and the haunting ruins of what was once the most spectacular of them all, Witley Court, built out of the massive personal wealth to be made from industrialisation.

The Worcestershire Way runs down the western edge, crossing the Abberley Hills whose wooded slopes rise to some 900 feet. In the middle ages Woodbury Hill was twice occupied by Owain Glendwr during his revolt against the English king, and later by the Duke of Buckingham in his rebellion against Richard III, events which remind us that this was border country, scene of much fighting and bloodshed before England and Wales united in peace.

East of the river lies Kidderminster, one of Worcestershire's largest towns, long famous for carpet manufacturing and, more recently, for the Severn Valley Railway.

(Above) Elgar's Birthplace, Lower Broadheath. The composer spent his first two years here before moving to Worcester

(Opposite page) Dowles Brook in the Wyre Forest, regular haunt of dippers, kingfishers and grey wagtails

THE ABBERLEY HILLS
AND THE SEVERN

Among the many listed buildings in 'black-and-white' Ombersley are two cruck houses, the Dower House and the Kings Arms where Charles II may have lodged after the battle of Worcester. He would have been safe: the manor was held by the Sandys family, fierce Royalists, whose influence on the village may be judged from the elegant George IV 'estate' church, built in the landscaped grounds of Ombersley Court, and the family mausoleum occupying part of the chancel, all that survives of the medieval church.

(Top right) Ombersley High Street, from St Andrew's churchyard

(Bottom right) Westwood Park, built as a hunting lodge in the late 1500s, altered and enlarged in the following century

(Left) The 400-year-old, half-timbered dovecote at Hawford, near Ombersley

(Opposite page) The Kings Arms, Ombersley

23

THE ABBERLEY HILLS
AND THE SEVERN

(Left) Elmley Lovett: site of a deserted medieval village. In Domesday one priest, fourteen villagers and fifteen smallholders lived here. St Michael's is in the background

(Opposite page) Redstone Rock, near Stourport, once a hermitage, later used as a cider house, a school and a number of rock dwellings

(Below) One of the county's small handful of wine producers, the award-winning Astley Vineyards, near Stourport. The Benedictines made wine here in the middle ages

Stourport-on-Severn, the town which owes its existence to the cutting of the Staffordshire and Worcestershire Canal in the 1760s

THE ABBERLEY HILLS AND THE SEVERN

The Court and church at Great Witley bear remarkable testimony to individual opulence. The manor was bought in the 17th century by a prosperous nail manufacturer whose descendants transformed the Jacobean residence into a great country house. Sold in the 1830s to the heir to the massive Dudley fortune, the great house was turned into a palace where royalty and aristocracy were regularly entertained. After a disastrous fire in 1937 the buildings fell into ruins until English Heritage stepped in and began restoration work. The adjacent St Michael's, started in 1733, was fashioned into England's finest baroque church, elegantly flamboyant - and completely unscathed by the fire.

(Above) Witley Court

(Right) Great Witley Church

(Left) The south doorway at Holt Church

(Opposite page) Winter frost, near Heightington

The clock tower between Abberley and Woodbury Hills is a surprising landmark: Victorian Gothic and over 160 feet high, it is visible for miles. Locally it is known as Jones's Folly, built in the 1880s by Joseph Jones who had bought the Italianate mansion, Abberley Hall, with money made from Lancashire cotton. Over the years the debate has been about his motives for such a tower in so rural a setting - a timekeeper for his farm labourers, a memorial to his wife or an attempt to keep up with his aristocratic neighbours at Witley Court?

(Above) Frozen pool, near Abberley

(Right) Abberley Hall clock tower

(Opposite page) Abberley Hills

No county is richer than Worcestershire in secret hiding places and Harvington Hall is widely regarded as England's finest Catholic stronghold. Moated and mellow, all gables and chimneys, this timber-framed medieval H-plan house was bought in the 16th century by a rich Protestant lawyer, and later enlarged and equipped with a variety of ingenious hiding places for Catholic priests. Among them was Father Wall who was hung at Worcester, the last man to be put to death for his faith.

(Right) The moated Harvington Hall

(Below right) Chaddesley Corbett Church, the only one in England to be dedicated to St Cassian

(Left) Village street, Chaddesley Corbett, one of the county's prettiest

(Opposite page) River Severn at Bewdley, once a busy inland port

THE ABBERLEY HILLS
AND THE SEVERN

Victoria Bridge which carries the Severn Valley Railway across the river

The restored station at Upper Arley

Before there were bridges there were ferries, and these have played a crucial part in communications over the centuries. Twenty ferries across the Severn have been identified and some survived up to the Second World War, Upper Arley both the most northerly and the last to operate.The coming of the train changed lives and landscape. The Severn Valley Line was opened in 1862 and the Severn Valley Railway, Britain's premier steam railway, gives the best feel of those earlier days on the journey between Kidderminster and Bridgnorth.

(Opposite page) The Severn at Upper Arley, a delightful riverside village where once a chain ferry operated

THE ABBERLEY HILLS AND THE SEVERN

The mills and chimneys of busy Kidderminster are abundant evidence of an industrial past when this was the world's leading centre for carpet manufacturing. In contrast, nearby Wolverley is tucked away in unspoilt countryside and overflowing with character, every building inviting inspection, the old school, endowed in 1620, the pound and cave dwellings cut out of red sandstone, and the picturesque cottages leading up to the church. In Kidderminster there is a statue of Rowland Hill, founder in 1840 of the modern postal system; but no such honour for the innovative printer and typefounder, John Baskerville, born in Wolverley in 1706.

(Left) The red-brick church of St John the Baptist, dominating the village of Wolverley

(Below left) The Music Room, Wolverley, one of the Sebright School buildings

(Right) St Mary's Church, Kidderminster, standing above the Staffordshire and Worcestershire Canal

(Opposite page) Slingfield Mill, owned by the carpet manufacturers, Brinton's

THE FOREST OF FECKENHAM
AND NORTH-EAST WORCESTERSHIRE

The line of hills crested by the North Worcestershire Way provides the county with a natural northern boundary. It was not always so. Dudley was for centuries part of Worcestershire, and the county once extended up the east side of what is now Birmingham. Today the ridge from Clent to Barnt Green acts as a green shield against creeping urbanisation and symbolises the transition from city to countryside. It is too easy to pigeonhole this area as Worcestershire's 'urbanised' north. The true picture is far more varied. The towns of Bromsgrove, Droitwich and Redditch all have some evidence of their ancient origins, though of their three main traditional industries only needlemaking survives, the relics of saltmining, a feature in Droitwich since Roman times, and nailmaking now found largely in the area's excellent museums.

In between these well-contained centres of population and light industry are numerous rural villages and hamlets, some barely changed in centuries; and pockets of ancient woodland survive from former times when much of the area was covered by the Royal Forest of Feckenham, the hunting ground of kings, one of whose keepers was the literary giant, Geoffrey Chaucer. This, too, is the area that boasts the county's most famous literary son, A E Housman; and bears witness to a strong involvement in the Gunpowder Plot and a resilient Catholic presence.

Climbing up the Midland plateau from Worcestershire's Severn Valley proved a tremendous challenge for the canal and railway engineers. The famously steep Lickey Incline and unique flight of locks at Tardebigge are wonderful reminders of their skill and ingenuity.

(Above) Outdoor market at the Kingfisher Centre, Redditch

(Opposite page) Clent Hills: the far-from-ancient standing stones, erected to 'improve' the landscape

*(Opposite page) The old
stone packhorse bridge at
Shell, a hamlet on the
Lower Saltway which ran
between Droitwich and
Stratford*

*Droitwich Spa, an ancient
salt town whose centre
has benefited from a
sensitive facelift*

There were saltmakers in Droitwich in prehistoric times; but today's natural brine - its strength rivalled only by the Dead Sea - draws people not to drink but to float in it. Brine baths were first opened in the 1830s and the town's subsequent development into a fashionable spa was rapid. The old baths have gone but a new brine bath was opened in 1985, the first new spa facility in Britain this century. The town has seen a lot of new housing in recent decades but three medieval churches, a little landscaped stream and half-timbered buildings at jaunty angles make this an attractive centre.

Himbleton Church, its bell-turret a reminder of the wealth of the county's surviving black-and-white half-timbering

Worcestershire played a major role in the Gunpowder Plot, several conspirators coming from the high proportion of Catholic families in the county. In the north-east there was a tight network of Roman Catholic houses - Badgecourt, Cooksey, Harvington, Hindlip, Huddington, Purshall, Rushock, Spetchley and the controlling centre, Grafton. At Huddington Court the Wyntour family was heavily involved in the plot. Thomas was the man who recruited Guy Fawkes and, later, his own reluctant brother; and Huddington was where the final arrangements were made, arms and munitions stored, and the dispirited plotters fled. Trying to escape across Worcestershire, they were captured near the border, tried and put to death. Despite continuing persecution, however, most Catholic families kept to the old faith.

The tiny semi-detached Baptist Chapel at Stock Green with its own burial ground

(Below left) The late-12th-century limestone lectern in Crowle Church, rescued from the churchyard and restored in the last century

(Below) Huddington Court, a serenely beautiful medieval manor house

Despite changes in recent years Inkberrow has retained much of its character. The little village green is flanked by brick and timber-framed houses and by The Old Bull, the model for the pub in *The Archers* , the long-running radio serial set firmly in the heart of Worcestershire. Particularly grotesque gargoyles adorn the porch of St Peter's Church, and inside there is some clever carving on one of the vestry screens by a member of the Bromsgrove Guild. Mindful perhaps of the church's connection with Charles I - he stayed at the vicarage on his way to the battle of Naseby, leaving behind a book of military maps - a space has been left between the head and shoulders of that ill-fated monarch.

(Right) St Peter's, Inkberrow

(Below) Sheltering from the sun: sheep near Grafton Wood, Grafton Flyford

(Opposite page) A summer evening at The Old Bull, Inkberrow

(Left) Characteristically Worcestershire: Bow Brook, Feckenham, a little stream winding through a forgotten corner of a field - yet only a mile or so from the highways of Redditch

(Opposite page) High Street, Feckenham

Feckenham is a rich mix of half-timbered, red-brick and whitewashed buildings, including some fine Georgian houses; and strict planning has helped it keep its historical shape and appearance. In the middle ages it was a thriving market centre and the seat of jurisdiction for the Royal Forest of Feckenham which stretched at one time from Evesham to Belbroughton and from Worcester to Alcester. Royal visits were frequent for the king owned the rights to hunt and the 'beasts of the chase' included wolves, badgers and deer, wild boar, martens and otters. A courthouse stood near the church to administer forest law - often harshly.

(Above) Village cricket at Feckenham, Holy Trinity in the background

(Right) Feckenham: a former needle factory, now a private house

THE FOREST OF FECKENHAM AND NORTH-EAST WORCESTERSHIRE

The old market town of Bromsgrove has long been the focal point for the villages and hamlets in the surrounding farmland. Recent years have seen pedestrianisation, new housing and a bypass, as well as a deserved reputation for literary and music events. But the new and the old rub shoulders. The fine medieval church still stands proud, in the churchyard two famous gravestones to the men blown to bits by the unfortunately named tank engine *Surprise*. The High Street's upper facades are mostly Georgian and once a year the ancient Court Leet is brought to life with a parade and re-enactment of old duties, such as ale-tasting. There remains some evidence of the nail industry which employed so many for so long; and flourishing still is Bromsgrove School, founded over 400 years ago.

Hanbury Church, wonderfully sited on a wooded mound with glorious views extending – on good days – to Bredon and the Cotswolds

(Right) The old steps leading to Bromsgrove's medieval sandstone church

(Far right) Bromsgrove High Street

(Below) Hanbury Hall, built in 1701and noted for its painted hall and ceiling and the separately housed Long Room, orangery and ice house

(Below right) The chain shop at Avoncroft Museum of Buildings which has rescued and re-erected a range of buildings from the middle ages to the 1940s

The country's longest flight of narrow locks - thirty achieve a rise of 217 feet on a 2.5-mile stretch of the Worcester-Birmingham Canal - gives the hamlet of Tardebigge its fame. In former days the canal was a busy working highway; now the traffic is all to do with leisure. Thirty years ago its big neighbour Redditch, the county's second town, was run-down and overcrowded; but New Town designation in 1964 led to redevelopment in a remarkably green environment. Where possible the new was grafted onto the old, for Redditch has a long past, settled by Saxons, later by Cistercians who built Bordesley Abbey, and later still by needlemakers who made its name famous throughout the world.

(Right) Redditch Market in the Kingfisher Centre

(Left) The Worcester-Birmingham Canal at Tardebigge

(Right) Forge Mill, restored to full working order. Sited in Arrow Valley Park, near the remains of Bordesley Abbey, it houses the National Needle Museum

(Opposite page) The slender baroque-type tower and 135-foot needle spire of St Bartholomew's Church, Tardebigge, visible for miles

(Below) The wooded slopes of the Lickey Hills, part of Worcestershire's green northern barrier

(Opposite page) Bear Hill, Alvechurch, an historic village with a good range of architectural styles, including much traditional and half-timbered redbrick

(Below) DraytonPool, typical of the quiet unspoilt hamlets around Belbroughton

(Below left) A memorial to the industry which earned the large and pleasant village of Belbroughton a worldwide reputation

Protected by the Clents and Lickeys much of the character of this corner of the county has survived. Small streams flow rapidly here and their power has been harnessed to effective purpose. The damming of Barnet Brook in its passage through Belbroughton enabled scythemakers to build up an international reputation until the end of the old industry in 1968. Alvechurch had its own mayor and Court Leet by the 1190s, and a summer palace for the bishops. By the 16th century things had changed: 'Plate none, goods none, preachers none, schools none'. But in recent years the aim has been to improve and to restore.

THIS HAMMER WAS MADE BY C.C.BRADLEY & SONS OF SYRACUSE U.S.A c.1897, AND USED FOR PLANISHING IN THE LOCAL NASH SCYTHE WORKS UNTIL 1968. DONATED BY MR D.COOPER OF DRAYTON FORGE, IT WAS SITED HERE BY BELBROUGHTON HISTORY SOCIETY AND PARISH COUNCIL IN COMMEMORATION OF THE VILLAGE'S INDUSTRIAL HERITAGE. UNVEILED BY MR WILFRID SAUNDERS, NASH WORKS FORMER MANAGER, 8TH MAY 1995

THE RIVER AVON

The vale of Evesham is blessed with some of the richest soil in the land and watered by the Avon which enters quietly from Warwickshire and meanders its way round Evesham and Pershore before joining the Severn at Tewkesbury.

This fertile area has been known for centuries for its extensive fruit orchards and market gardens. Spring heralds mile upon mile of stunning blossom, pink and yellow and white; by autumn the same trees are all mellow golds and russetts.

Near the county's southern boundary Bredon Hill rises dramatically from low ground, an isolated outpost of the Cotswolds, offering wonderful panoramic views across the Severn Vale to the west and north over the Avon towards the lower wooded hills of the Lenches.

Around the bottom of the hill is a string of picturesque villages, but the whole area is a handsome mix of traditional domestic architecture: half-timbered thatched cottages and houses of brick and, in the south, of yellow Cotswold stone.

The three main centres offer contrasting attractions: the elegant Georgian facades of Pershore with its strangely truncated abbey; the rich variety of medieval buildings in busy Evesham, including the Bell Tower and the Almonry in the abbey precinct, the Round House and Old Grammar School in the town; and at the foot of the Cotswolds the majestic High Street of Broadway, one of England's most beautiful villages.

(Above) Hampton Ferry, the country's only rope-drawn ferry - still a useful way to Evesham's shops

(Opposite page) The Banbury Stone near the top of Bredon Hill

53

Pershore Old Bridge, built by the monks in the 14th century and the only remaining monastic bridge over the Worcestershire Avon

The small market town of Pershore stands on the banks of a beautiful stretch of the Avon. An important centre for the fruit and vegetable trade - and known especially for its plums - it boasts England's only specialist horticultural college. In such a rural setting the elegance of the town's Georgian architecture may come as a surprise. The wide main street and square are lined mainly with 18th-century houses of brick, several with cast-iron balconies and elaborate doorways; and its former coaching inns, distinguishable by their high arched entrances, underline the prosperity the town enjoyed when it stood on the main London to Holyhead route. Pershore's story begins many centuries earlier, however, with the founding of the great abbey, probably in the 7th century, around which the town grew and prospered. In Norman times there was a lot of rebuilding but when the abbey was dissolved in 1539 much of the building was demolished, leaving only a stump of the nave, the transepts and the chancel. Even so, it is widely regarded as one of the Midlands' finest churches, its 14th-century lantern tower particularly beautiful and possibly the work of the man who built Salisbury Cathedral.

(Above left) Pirton Church with the county's only aisled half-timbered tower, probably 14th-century

(Above) Pershore Abbey, all that remains of the extensive monastic buildings which once dominated the town

Bridge Street, Pershore, one of the many Georgian houses

THE RIVER AVON

(Left) Bredon tithe barn, the only aisled barn in Worcestershire and the second largest in England

(Opposite page) Massively impressive: the two porches of Bredon tithe barn

Massive and isolated, Bredon Hill rises abruptly to nearly 1000 feet out of the plain surrounding it. There was a settlement here in prehistoric times; and from it there are extensive views over the vales of the Avon and Severn, the 'coloured counties' immortalised by Housman in *A Shropshire Lad*. The villages encircling Bredon were settled by Saxons and the fertile land they found has been put to full use in the production of fruit and vegetables. The area's unspoilt beauty has inspired many writers, among them John Drinkwater: 'God laughed when he made Grafton, / That's under Bredon's Hill, / A jewel in a jewelled plain ... '.

(Right) The Queen Elizabeth Inn at Elmley Castle, commemorating the queen's stay in 1575 with the lord of the manor

(Left) Great Comberton churchyard

(Opposite page) On the edge of Bredon village the gently meandering Avon meets the M5 motorway

(Below) The Anglo-Saxon cross head at Cropthorne Church

Memorials to the Dingley family at Cropthorne

The picture-postcard village of Cropthorne lies on an old drovers' road where up to 400 Welsh cattle would rest on their way to London. The Norman church houses two treasures. An Anglo-Saxon cross head - carved over a thousand years ago and richly decorated with birds, beasts and foliage - is on display in the north aisle. Resting in painted splendour are Francis Dingley, his wife and nineteen children; but a later Dingley was buried more discreetly, murdered by his brother in a bitter feud which hastened the family's catastrophic decline.

The great Benedictine abbey at Evesham, founded in 701, was one of the country's richest religious houses, and crowds of pilgrims flocked to its various shrines. Ruthless demolition at the Reformation and long-term looting have left only the wonderful Bell Tower, the building known as the Almonry and Abbot Reginald's Gateway. On 4 August 1265 the Barons' War ended here when rebel forces led by Simon de Montfort were heavily defeated by Prince Edward. Parts of de Montfort's dismembered body were buried beneath the high altar; but the seeds of parliamentary democracy had been sown.

(Above) Evesham: All Saints (left), St Lawrence (centre) and, behind them, the Bell Tower

(Left) The site of the battle of Evesham, marking the end of the Barons' War in 1265

(Opposite page) The Almonry Museum, Evesham's heritage centre

Long before the monasteries were dissolved fruit growing and market gardening were the main occupations, fostered by the abbots of Evesham and Pershore and thus their lasting legacy to the area known as 'The Garden of England'. The variety of fruit grown three centuries ago is staggering: 82 types of apples, according to John Rea writing in 1676, 69 kinds of pears, 44 of plums, 35 of peaches, 24 of cherries, 11 of nectarines and 6 of figs. The capital of this fertile vale is the country town of Evesham which continues to market its products and service its villages.

(Above) The Norman gateway, built by Abbot Reginald, which once connected the abbey cemetery with the town

(Left) The Avon at Evesham

(Opposite page) As well as its market gardening the peaceful village of Offenham in the Vale of Evesham boasts one of the country's five original maypoles

(Left) On a clear day Broadway Tower offers views over a dozen counties

(Opposite page) Flea Bank, Broadway: 16th-century cottages known as Shakespeare Cottages. Condemned in 1930 they were restored in the following decade

In the last century Broadway attracted a number of leading Pre-Raphaelites and writers in search of the perfect English village. The mellow-stoned buildings flanking its long wide High Street fully justify their sentiments: despite changes and increased traffic the village has retained its Cotswold character and thrives as a tourist centre. Entering from the north there is a view of Broadway Tower, a 65-foot folly built by the Earl of Coventry two centuries ago; entering from the south, down steeply winding Fish Hill, visitors can only marvel at the skill of the stagecoach driver when Broadway was on a main London route.

(Right) Gordon Russell Ltd, famous for furniture design

(Left) Upper High-Street, Broadway, on the left the teddy bear museum

The Lenches nestle quietly among farmed and wooded hills north of Evesham: Ab, Atch, Church, Rous and Sherrif's. The area is rich in black-and-white cottages and there are interesting churches at Rous Lench and Church Lench. The little Baptist chapel at Atch Lench, a place of worship for over 150 years, has an unusually large burial ground which speaks of continuity: most of the buried bear the name Bomford.

(Left) Toy Cottage, Church Lench, said to have once housed a family of fourteen

(Far left) 12th-century relief of Christ above the south door of Rous Lench Church

(Opposite page) The much-filmed medieval pub at Bretforton, the Fleece Inn, host to an annual asparagus auction

(Below) An eye on the camera: cattle near the hamlet of Abberton

THE MALVERN HILLS
AND THE SEVERN PLAIN

For centuries the Malverns presented a formidable western barrier against successive waves of invaders. The pre-Cambrian range is the county's most striking natural feature, a ridge of granite reaching almost 1400 feet, bare and rugged in stark contrast to the lushness of surrounding meadow and woodland. The hills rise steeply out of low land on the east, almost like a child's drawing, with crowning peaks at each end. Now they are crossed and encircled by roads and pierced by tunnel for the railway; but impressive earthworks of Iron-Age forts survive and the centuries-old practice of lighting beacons on the tops is still very much alive.

For so many, in this and surrounding counties, the Malverns define the horizon. From them, in turn, are the most commanding views - north to the Wrekin, south to Bristol, east over the Midland plain, and west towards Wales. To see them is to be reminded of Elgar - who is buried in Little Malvern at the foot of his 'beloved hills'; and of that May morning some six centuries ago when William Langland lay down and dreamed of a better society which he wrote about in his Vision of Piers Plowman.

The Malverns' eastern slopes protect a line of villages linked to Great Malvern whose Victorian flourish owed much to the recognition of the purity of its spring water. The town's old priory has outstanding medieval stained glass and encaustic tiles unparalleled in England. There are some fine manor houses in this area - Madresfield, Birtsmorton and Croome, for example; and below the hills on the Severn plain are numerous attractive villages and the market town of Upton-on-Severn, once a prosperous port.

(Above) Priory Gateway, Great Malvern

(Opposite page) The Herefordshire Beacon, crowned by British Camp, an Iron-Age fortress

Malvern Priory stands today because in 1541, when most of the monastic buildings had been pulled down, the local people bought the priory church for £20. It may have originated in a Saxon hermitage in what was then a wooded wilderness. It was formally recognised as a Benedictine house in 1085 and solid Norman pillars survive in a predominantly Perpendicular church, the result of major rebuilding in the 15th century. The new enlarged windows were filled with a collection of stained glass which is the priory's particular glory; and the 1200 medieval tiles, locally made with some 90 different designs, are the finest in the country. The Malvern Hills, the priory's majestic backdrop, are amongst the oldest in the world. At their highest point the Worcestershire Beacon reaches nearly 1400 feet; and further south on this nine-mile range the Herefordshire Beacon is crowned with impressive Iron-Age earthworks.

(Above) The ornate exterior of Malvern Priory, with its dominating 15th-century tower

(Left) 15th-century wall tiles in Malvern Priory

(Opposite page) Great Malvern and its centrepiece, the priory

71

THE MALVERN HILLS
AND THE SEVERN PLAIN

(Left) The Morgan: style and craftsmanship characterise the last coachbuilt car in the world

(Below) Great Malvern railway station, restored to its Victorian splendour

A couple of centuries ago a book on the beneficial effects of Malvern water by John Wall, physician and founder of Worcester's porcelain works, began Great Malvern's transformation from an unknown village to a fashionable health resort. Now the pure water is bottled and sold in supermarkets, and it is the town's oldest asset, the hills, that beckon visitors and the retired. This is also the home of the Morgan, the unrealised dream of many an adult; a restored Victorian railway station whose platform restaurant sells anything but the traditional BR sandwich; and a theatre and annual festival initially supported by George Bernard Shaw.

(Opposite page) 'Hills draw like leaves,/ And stronger sometimes, holding out their hands/ to pull you from the vile flats up to them'. (From Aurora Leigh *by Elizabeth Barrett Browning who lived at the foot of the Malverns for some years)*

St Giles, Little Malvern, once the church of a Benedictine priory founded in the 12th century. Little Malvern Court incorporates the refectory, all that survived of the priory

(Left) Castlemorton Common from the southern end of the Malverns

(Opposite page) The gently rolling Suckley Hills, lying near the Herefordshire border in arable and fruit-growing country

Kempsey has always been a favoured place, out of Worcester but near enough to make use of its facilities. The bishop had a palace here and he and his retinue were rowed down river to entertain the great of the land; and the number of servants' gravestones in the churchyard indicates a comfortable existence for many 19th-century parishioners. The church's fine five-light lancet east window proved irresistible to keen Victorians who organised copies in many another church. The chancel itself was brand new when Simon de Montfort heard mass here on the day of his defeat at Evesham, having stayed overnight with his friend the bishop.

(Left) Medieval stained glass in the chancel of St Mary the Virgin, Kempsey

(Opposite page) The old brick bridge and ford at Kempsey, a few miles south of Worcester

THE MALVERN HILLS AND THE SEVERN PLAIN

These days it is pleasure boats which moor at the riverside town of Upton-on-Severn. In the past the traffic was very different: substantial trading vessels reached this busy inland port, for a long time the only Severn crossing between Worcester and Gloucester. The old stone bridge was a gathering place for the watermen who sailed the trows - flat-bottomed barges unique to the Severn - and the bowhauliers who, before horse and towpath, pulled them upstream. The town was also an important staging post and the handsome Georgian inns and houses - including the White Lion, said to be the model for scenes in Fielding's *Tom Jones* - underline this 18th-century prosperity.

(Opposite page) 'The Pepperpot', Upton-on-Severn, a striking combination of 14th-century church tower and Continental-looking dome, cupola and lantern, added in the mid-18th century

(Right) Ornate guttering at Hanley Castle Church

Hanley Castle: only the moat of King John's castle remains, but the village is rich in old buildings - a fine church, black-and-white cottages, a timber-framed inn, almshouses and the original grammar school building, founded in 1544

The River Severn has shaped much of the county's development. Before the age of steam it was the main commercial highway; today it is a great source of pleasure, but its quick-flowing power and tendency to flood demand respect. Whole fields of cattle were swept away in 1811 when a storm caused the river to rise 25 feet above normal; floods destroyed Bewdley's old bridge in 1795 and Upton's comparatively new one in 1872; and the county cricket ground at Worcester continues to suffer - though not perhaps as much as in the past when rowing on it was not uncommon and one man claimed to have caught a fish from the pavilion steps.

The pride of Ripple: 15th-century misericords, some of the best in Britain, celebrating activities on the land, month by month

(Above) March - sowing

(Top right) August - reaping

(Middle) September - corn for malting

(Bottom right) October - acorns for pigs

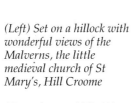

(Left) Set on a hillock with wonderful views of the Malverns, the little medieval church of St Mary's, Hill Croome

(Opposite page) The River Severn at Upton

THE TEME VALLEY

ne of England's prettiest rivers runs through this beautiful and unspoilt corner of Worcestershire. The Teme, fast-flowing on its journey from mid-Wales but never very deep, passes beneath the old Powick bridge, site of the first skirmish in the Civil Wars, just before joining its big sister, the Severn, below Worcester.

Rolling hills, wooded and farmed, lush meadows, orchards and hopyards, all characterise this richly varied area bordering on Herefordshire and Shropshire, a territory of ancient strife but now tranquil and wild only in its natural beauty.

Perry, a winey drink made from particular varieties of tart pears, was a favourite here; and the number of surviving cider presses tucked away on farms is evidence of a once thriving industry. Hop growing goes back nearly three-and-a-half centuries, becoming more specialised and developed in the nineteenth century. Hops surge into growth in high summer when the cherry and apple and damson blossom is becoming a memory. Gone are the days when whole families of hop pickers descended on the area for the season, but some of the older type of hop kilns can still be seen.

Tenbury, the area's only town, lies right on the Shropshire border. Once a coaching stage on the main route between London and North Wales, it has long been known as 'the town in the orchard'. It has a fine bridge and an interesting church and its main streets present an attractive mixture of half-timbered, Georgian and Victorian buildings, including the house once occupied by Henry Hickman, a pioneer in anaesthesia.

(Above) Sundial in Mamble churchyard, tucked away near the Shropshire border

(Opposite page) Standing like a beacon, Rock Church - appropriately named St Peter's

The opening skirmish in the English Civil War took place around Powick Bridge when a Parliamentary force under Colonel Fiennes accidentally stumbled across Prince Rupert and his cavalry, resting on a hot September afternoon in 1642. Fiennes had been shadowing a royal convoy of silver plate and Rupert was sent to escort it to the king at Shrewsbury. The encounter was short but sharp, with casualities on both sides; but it was the Parliamentarians who fled in confusion. Nine years later, at the final battle, the old stone bridge was again in the thick of the action. A section was destroyed and bullet marks in the church nearby give further proof of the full-scale encounter. This time Cromwell's men achieved a crushing defeat, forcing Charles to flee for his life.

(Right) The tithe barn at Leigh, the largest remaining full-cruck building in the country

(Right) The River Teme at Knightwick where sandmartins swoop after damselflies as they hover above the water's surface

(Left) Powick Mills. There were mills on this site at the time of the Domesday Survey

(Opposite page) Old Powick Bridge, near Worcester. A 'new' iron bridge was built a century and a half ago

The Shelsleys - Beauchamp, Kings and Walsh - lie in a secluded valley of the River Teme running between Woodbury Hill and Clifton Ridge, all steep lanes, wooded hillsides, isolated farmhouses and hopyards and orchards. All the more surprising therefore is the fact that for four days a year this most peaceful corner of the county plays host to people who travel from all over the world to compete in the oldest motoring speed event on earth, the Shelsley Walsh Hill Climb. It was started by the Midland Automobile Club in 1905 on a track at the Court House - from where exactly three centuries earlier High Sherrif Walsh set out to capture the Gunpowder Plot conspirators.

(Above) Shelsley Beauchamp, its church standing among hopyards

(Right) An orchard on Penn Hill, near Pensax

(Opposite page) The tiny church of Shelsley Walsh has one of the most beautiful interiors in the county. Amongst its treasures are a magnificent 15th-century rood screen, a fine carved roof and a tomb entirely of wood

Rock Church stands 600 feet above sea level in the village reputed to be the coldest in the county. Alongside its elaborately carved doorway and its chancel arch - one of the best examples of Norman decorative sculpture in England - there are the village stocks and whipping post, reminders of harsher days when those found guilty of misdemeanours were punished in public. Outside the church, on the north side of the chancel wall, is a series of grooves, made, it is claimed, in 1405 by Owain Glendwr's men when preparing for battle against Henry IV of England. Aided by the French, Glendwr marched onto Worcester which he plundered and burnt.

The north entrance to Rock Church, the county's largest Norman village church

(Opposite page) Grazing cattle at the foot of Woodbury Hill

(Left) The hop-clad timber porch of Stockton-on-Teme Church

(Opposite page) The fruits of field and orchard: harvest display at Clifton-on-Teme

(Right) Hopyards (Worcestershire's word for hopfields) near Tenbury Wells

THE TEME VALLEY

The hopyard and the cherry orchard are characteristic of the narrow Teme Valley and both crops require a lot of attention. 'Hops be faddy mortals ... you've got to humour them beggars', wrote Francis Brett Young in his novel *Far Forest*. Though under threat from the fashion for lagers and imported drinks, hops are still important to the valley's economy. For generations picking was done largely by hand and the pickers - mainly women and children - would descend from Birmingham, the Black Country and from Wales for six weeks' hard work, usually in primitive conditions. Yet many hop pickers have looked back with affection on these times.

THE TEME VALLEY

(Right) The Ship Inn, Tenbury Wells

Down the centuries the ancient border town of Tenbury has experienced a remarkably peaceful existence. Over the bridge from Shropshire, along the road from Herefordshire, it was once a coaching stage on the London-Holyhead road. When saline springs were discovered in the 19th century it had hopes of becoming a leading spa: buildings to house baths and a pump room were erected and 'Wells' tagged on to the old name. But an attempt to popularise the place came too late - spas had gone out of fashion - and Tenbury returned to the role it plays best, the tranquil centre of beautiful hop- and fruit-growing country.

(Opposite page) Further refreshment: Teme Passage, Tenbury Wells

(Below right) The bizarre pagoda-shaped building erected to house Tenbury's water-cure facilities in 1862

(Below) Once a railway station, now a garden centre - Newnham Bridge

But come with me where change has seen no change;
Where unspoiled woods kneel to the water's edge ...
These banks where kingcups grow have never changed
And in the sullen murmur of the stream
Is held the music of eternity ...

Joe Hunt, from *Severn*

*(Opposite page) Kyre
Pool, Kyre Park, grounds
landscaped by Capability
Brown*

*Seen from the motorway:
Panorama Tower at
Croome Park . The estate
is being restored by the
National Trust*

INDEX

References in italics refer to illustrations